MW01489968

Glad to be Living Life

Creating more enjoyment in your life

By Matthew D. Mohr

Library of Congress Control Number: 2002093853
ISBN 0-9709251-2-3
MG
Printed in the United States of America

Additional copies may be ordered from:

Dacotah Paper Co.

P.O. Box 2727

Fargo, ND 58102

(800) 323-7583

FORWARD

Over the course of a lifetime, many people have passed through my life. Of particular importance to my public speaking and writing abilities were Joan Humphrey, Melinda Kramer, and Sarah Honea Ring. All three women inspired me to reach for the best within myself. All encouraged me to pursue speaking, writing, and teaching for the benefit of others.

A special thank you to my Executive Assistant, Marcia Hagen, for doing all the work necessary for the successful publishing of this work.

DEDICATION

For everyone who has encouraged me to enjoy
life to the fullest and helped me to step up to the
plate and take a whole hearted swing at the ball.
Most especially, I thank my mother Marcia Mohr,
my grandmother Ruth Erickson, my three children
Benjamin, Caleb and Berea, and all the
employees of Dacotah Paper Co. You all help me
live a wonderful life, and most of you exhibit the
joy in life which God intends for us to live.

INTRODUCTION

Each of us have a different perspective concerning the value of life and what constitutes living successfully.

Throughout this book we will explore various aspects of life. Our objective will be to establish ways for your life to become richer and more enjoyable.

As we explore together you should develop a greater sense of meaning for your life. Wherever you find yourself today, a better life can be yours as long as you are willing to open your mind and open your senses to the world around us. Throughout the book, we will uncover many ways to appreciate life and live more fully.

Table of Contents

Table of Contents (continued)

Table of Contents (continued)

Chapter 1

SECOND CHANCES

You can only be sure of an opportunity the first time.

Most all of us have read stories or learned of someone who had a near death experience. These stories typically are meant to inspire us to better appreciate our lives. Those who do get a second chance to live, typically try to change to live a better life. When disaster does strike, not everyone will get a second chance, and not everyone will be inspired to live their lives to the fullest.

On March 20, 1998, I suffered a massive stroke, a right cerebral vascular attack to be more precise. A stroke is caused by a blood clot in the brain, or the bursting of a blood vessel in the brain. In either case, the victim faces some brain damage. In fact, stroke is the number one cause of disability among adults in the United States today.

My stroke was caused by a blood clot, resulting in a large area of damage to the right hemisphere of my brain. Fortunately for me, MeritCare hospital in Fargo, ND was pioneering the use of the clot busting drug tissue plasminogen activator (tPA for short) and I escaped death. Spending several weeks in the hospital only gave me a start to the physical and mental rebuilding which was needed. My life was spared by employing the most advanced methods of modern medicine. Only a few short years ago, the result of this stroke would have been almost certain death, or if not death, at best, significant mental and physical disability.

Of course, this major medical event helped me to evaluate the significance which life or death would have had on me and my loved ones.

As we pursue the building of a more enjoyable life together in this book, please remember that I did get a second chance.

Chapter 2

ON STROKES

Stroke Facts:

- ➤ Stroke is a devastating affliction.
- ➤ Our medical community has few definite answers about the widespread causes of stroke.
- ➤ Stroke effects all ages, not just the elderly.
- ➤ Stroke is the number one cause of disability in the United States.
- ➤ More than 700,000 Americans suffer from a stroke each year.

Every 3.3 minutes someone dies from a stroke.

Warning Signals of Stroke:

- ➤ Sudden speech difficulties – words don't come out right or are mumbled
- ➤ Loss of sight in one or both eyes – having "blind spots"
- ➤ Sudden severe head ache
- ➤ Weakness / paralysis especially in one side of the body

Chapter 3

LIFE OR DEATH

Live life or you'll miss your chance at life.

One must ponder death to fully appreciate life. Life or death are not the only options available to us. A person can be alive but not really live life.

Recovering from a stroke is not easy, often people would say; "You are alive, think of the alternative."

Thinking of the alternative (death) did not create any cheerful feelings.

Initially, I was certainly afraid of dying, but as time went on, I realized it was not death which was feared, but the possibility of having to go through life without really being able to enjoy each moment.

Death may be viewed by some as a better result of an illness or accident than not being able to really live life after the illness or accident occurs. Few of us really would choose death over life. But if you are given the chance to live, you should enjoy your life. Illness, accident, or not, you have a lot to live for.

Melody was an attractive, smart, enthusiastic young college student and friend who tended to

12

go after every activity with gusto. She decided to try a parachute jump. She learned the skills necessary for a successful first jump, but on that fateful first jump, her chute failed to open and she was killed.

Had Melody lived, she no doubt would have embraced life as vigorously as possible. Melody did not get a second chance. Perhaps she was fortunate since she was not placed alive in the position of complete physical or mental incapacity. Today all that is left of her are positive memories, and the echoes of the laughter heard only in the minds of her friends.

It is impossible to say how Melody would have reacted to physical or mental disability, but one must ponder if God's will for her death was a better result than her living a life as an invalid. Melody didn't have to slow down, but had she lived, she most likely would have done her best to charge forward faster than ever.

Perhaps you support euthanasia. After surviving a catastrophic medical situation it is hard to suggest that the option of choosing death would have created a better result.

Chapter 4

SLOW DOWN?

Once you accept less of yourself you get less from yourself.

Taking action is the only way to create results. Only by doing something can you move towards a more enjoyable life.

So many people think by doing less each day, becoming less demanding, or requiring a lower level of performance of themselves, will ultimately lead to a better life. Sorry, but slowing your life down and creating the desire to accomplish less will not give you a better life!

Where would we be if God decided to rest on the sixth day as well as the seventh? If, after day five, God would have decided he had done enough and He rested for the next two days, our world would be incomplete today.

If God would have decided to keep on working the seventh day just imagine what He might have created for us to enjoy!

Fortunately God knew when he created the best place for all of us, but He didn't stop working on us or our world. Everyday He helps us to become better through His teachings and our experiences.

We are all put on this earth to create good for ourselves and for our fellow man. Take away the hammer from a true builder and the builder will become bewildered and lost. For a true builder must create new places for the living, and his hammer is an extension of himself. Personally, as people asked me after my stroke if I had slowed down, and was taking life easy, it was simple to relate how after seven weeks of forced confinement in a hospital, my attitude about life became more determined than ever. In the process, I became more vocal and much less tolerant of laziness. Why settle for being less than one can be?

In the summer of 2002, we were building extra bedrooms above our garage. We picked Schmit Brothers Construction in Fargo, since we determined that they were the best company to do the job. One Sunday afternoon in July, it was raining, and as Richard Schmit, the business owner, drove by our house with his daughter he stopped, climbed a ladder and went up on the roof to help us secure our house from the rainstorm.

Richard is very successful, has a full schedule and a thriving business. He didn't need to be on our roof that Sunday. Undoubtedly a big part of his success comes from his direct involvement and concern for each project he undertakes. Many people in his position would have simply driven by our house that rainy Sunday. We can name a dozen other contractors we chose not to employ who probably wouldn't have considered helping us that rainy Sunday. Richard Schmit could have driven by, but he didn't. He is respected and successful because he does the job, cares about his customers, and is willing to do what is right.

No matter where you are in your life today, you know you can create a better life for yourself and those you love. The best in your life is yet to come as long as you strive forward to be all you can.

Chapter 5

ALL YOU CAN BE

A tree will always grow as tall as it can, so should you.

Part of enjoying life involves the feeling of accomplishment. We all strive for recognition, love and acceptance. As we create a better world we receive all three of these (recognition, love and acceptance) in return for what we have done.

The U.S. Army uses the slogan "be all you can be" in its advertising to draw recruits. This slogan hits at the heart of what we all want for ourselves. Why not be all we can be?

A builder uses cement, bricks and wood to create a bungalow. He feels pride in seeing his work create shelter for his fellow man.

As the builder watches a family move into their new home, seeing the love and pride in the eyes of the new family occupying the space he built, the builder knows he has done well with the choices he has made for his work. Over the years, each structure becomes a standing monument to the builders success.

The homes which stand the test of time provide a continued reminder of the builders good choice in his profession.

Chapter 6

YOUR WORK

America has grown to become the greatest nation through the unrelenting pride in the work of its people.

Regardless of the job you hold, who you work for, and how much you earn, you can, and should, recognize the benefits you receive from your work and the benefits you provide to society from your work.

Far too many people take their jobs for granted today. We have built a great economic society in America; almost everyone who has a job enjoys a very good lifestyle. We must teach our children the value of a good, honest days work.

Many business managers are questioning if Generation X will have the commitment or ability to keep our economy strong. Much of the fear comes from the realization our Generation X'ers have been told over and over how much their parents' work has interfered with their parents' lives. They have heard, family life would be great if Dad or Mom didn't have to go to work.

Your work provides you with some monetary income. This income regardless of its size, allows you to purchase some food, shelter and clothing. If your income is not what you desire, it is up to you to invest in yourself so you can enhance your income. This book and its ideas should help you appreciate your life's income pursuit.

A headline in our local newspaper read "Man dies under bridge." Sensational headlines for a small city. The article detailed how the man took shelter under the bridge eventually dying from exposure. If you have some sort of job, you probably aren't living under a bridge, so be thankful. Recognize the benefit of the shelter you have!

Possibly, just as the man who died under the bridge was about to expire, he may have thought; "maybe it would be a good idea for me to get a job." If he did think this, it was too late. Take a close look at your job, no doubt you will find some good in what you do. If you are unhappy with your job, take a closer look to discover the good.

A woman delivers cleaning chemicals as her job. She is frustrated by her paycheck plus the back breaking work, and becomes disillusioned. On Thursday she delivers a box of cleaner to the local hamburger stand. Later she learns four young children were hospitalized on Wednesday from eating contaminated meat in the hamburgers they bought at this hamburger stand. Friday she learns her two young sons ate hamburgers from the same place for lunch. Friday night, after their hamburger lunch purchased at this same stand, her children are well and have no illness. She remembers the cleaner she delivered killed the germs which cause the illness.

19

Perhaps this story never happened, and perhaps it never will. But we all have an important role in the jobs we do. If this delivery woman takes the right perspective about the value of her job, she will become a much happier person. Of course, it takes the right perspective to enjoy your work. Your general interest in life often is reflected in how you relate to the people around you and the enjoyment you discover in life.

Chapter 7

YOUR INTEREST

Dreams and desires created by curiosity often evolve into hours of happiness.

Everyone has different interests. One person can be thrilled to ride a carousel at the county fair, another may despise the carousel. How you respond to the various experiences you have during your life, how you view the world around you can provide welcome enjoyment or great frustration. The more interested you are in activities, the more you can expect people to be interested in you.

Some of the most enjoyable times Cynthia and I have shared are camping, canoeing and just generally enjoying the outdoors. We both are thrilled to see an Eagle tend to its nest. All around us are examples of natural beauty. By showing interest in the world around us, we learn to appreciate life and become more interesting people. We were all meant to share these interests with others.

Cynthia didn't realize when she suggested early in our relationship for us to go canoeing that she had uncovered one of my most inspirational activities. We canoed a lot during our courtship. We both seemed to love it, and found the time exciting and inspirational. One beautiful day we canoed a lake in Wisconsin. We spotted a magnificent Bald Eagle and watched it for hours. To this day that experience remains one of each of our most enjoyable life experiences. We didn't recognize it at the time, but through canoeing together our premarital romantic relationship was greatly enhanced.

One Sunday afternoon I found myself driving an automobile with a woman who at one time was very interested in life. Her interest fascinated me and seemed to match the innate curiosity for life of mine. The following repeats our "conversations" during this 3 hour trip.

M: That was a great trip, everyone seemed to have fun.

W: Yes, it was a good idea.

M: Traffic is moving really well through Minneapolis today.

W: It is Sunday.

M: I hope we don't see rain or bad weather.

W: It might snow, it's cold out.

M: Amazing how cold it got when last week it was in the 70's.

W: Can't do much about it.

M: I don't feel comfortable using the cruise control as it may be icy on the bridges, we don't need to end up in the ditch.

W: Oh.

M: Look at the huge goose in the water; sure seems to be a lot of birds around this year.

W: Um hum.

M: We sure have seen some beautiful birds on this trip, we are lucky to see them.

W: I guess so.

M: Funny-usually birds know when the weather is changing so they stay where it is warm.

W: Not all of them.

M: Do you have an idea when you want to stop and eat lunch?

W: It doesn't matter to me when or where.

M: How about restaurant A or B or C?

W: I don't care, just pick one and lets keep going.

M: Look at that old building, it looks like it may have been a store way back when.

W: Pretty small store.

M: It's probably 150 years old, so they probably didn't need a lot of space.

W: I guess not.

M: Wouldn't it be fascinating to be able to see just what it was like 150 years ago.

W: Maybe.

M: Think of what it would be like if you could live that long and see all the changes over time.

W: I don't want to live that long.

M: We should be back in Fargo in twenty minutes, we made good time today.

W: It's a long drive.

M: Do you want to stop anywhere in Fargo.

W: Just take me home.

M: Do you think we got much rain in Fargo today?

W: Who cares, it's no big deal anyway.

M: Have I done something to bother you?

W: No.

M: I've tried at least a dozen times to start a conversation with you today.

W: Not much that interested me.

Not much of a conversation for a three hour drive. Perhaps this is a little bit one-sided, but the essence of the day's events should be clear to you. How interested you are in the world often determines how interested you are in those around you and how interested those around you are in you! It is up to you to develop an interest in our world. Have you ever been stuck with someone who didn't have any enthusiasm or interest in life? No doubt if you have found yourself with an uninterested person you wondered how they could miss so much of the world's beauty.

A person who is not interested in much is usually pretty boring to be around. Interests are developed along with enthusiasm for the world around us. You can create interest in many things within yourself. As you become interested, you will become interesting.

Try looking around you more closely as you drive from one place to another. Ask a few questions about anything you see.

Chapter 8

YOUR WORLD

A successful person constantly looks forward to moving beyond the accomplishments of yesterday.

This world which we inhabit is an incredible place. We all tend to create our own 'space', and we all tend to create our own little world in our own space. How you view your world is a matter of your perspective.

While growing up, to my best friend and I, Fargo seemed like an awfully boring, small town. My father loved living here, which was hard to understand as an adolescent. Fortunately he shared his love by showing all of us in the family the hidden or not so hidden secrets of our city. He had a wealth of knowledge about the town from what businesses occupied what buildings, to who owned what land, to stories of street cars, river boats, floods, parades and long forgotten steam tunnels under ground.

As we learned to drive as high schoolers, many times my father told us the story of how he and my mother would walk rather than take the bus from college to the Fargo Theater. At that time, a bus ride would have cost 10 cents each. A bus ride for 10 cents seemed ridiculous when we had a car to drive! Would a 10 cent cost for a bus ride entice you to abandon your car today?

Over the years, my fascination with old steel safes grew as my father talked about the old huge walk-in safes which were once built. Why either of us cared about old safes is hard to know. One day a building which once housed my grandfather's employer became available for sale. While touring the building, a huge walk-in safe door protected an area just off the executive offices. It is likely that this was where my father grew to become fascinated with such a thing. Unfortunately he is gone, and the only thing to do is speculate about his reasons for his interest in old safes.

Another of my father's favorite stories revolved around what he called "the great flood". Most likely this was the flood which occurred in Fargo in 1943 or 1947. He told of how he canoed around the hospital and showed us where the water filled the main arteries of town. Such colossal stories of water in the streets were hard to believe until in 1997, when we experienced a similar flood, and until we discovered pictures of the "big flood" showing bridges over the water leading to the hospital and police patrolling the area in boats.

As children, we were forced to patiently listen to father's unbelievable stories. Now, years later, as we discover these stories were true, we have a much deeper appreciation for our community and a much richer understanding of our heritage.

Regardless of where you live you can uncover some aspect of history which is unique. These special historical tid-bits can add excitement to your life if you embrace them.

From boring, unbelievable tales of an uninteresting place, age has proven Fargo, and North Dakota in general, to be a fascinating, wonderful place to live and raise a family.

Temporary bridge leading to what was St. John's Hospital – 4th Street and 6th Avenue South, Fargo, ND during "the great flood".

Fargo Police patrolling during "the great flood".
This Red Owl Grocery Market was formerly
located in Fargo.

An early Fargo Flag Day Parade Float

An early Flag Day Parade on Broadway in Fargo.

More of Fargo during "the great flood."

More of Fargo during "the great flood."

Chapter 9

NEXT DOOR

What you have is only as good as your attitude about what you have.

Are you constantly looking over the fence at your neighbors grass with envy? Or are you looking over your fence with interest trying to learn how to better tend to your lawn? Perhaps a bit of both?

Certainly our neighbors grass looks greener than ours at times. But the right attitude is to pull the weeds in your lawn, tend to your lawn and make it the most beautiful lawn on the block. Such is the way of our lives.

There is a story of a man named Olaf who lived outside Dickinson, ND on a ranch he inherited from his father. His father had bought 150 acres of land for $1.00 per acre back when a dollar was worth something. All Olaf received from his father was this rocky, barren 150 acres of land. Despite the hard life of working the land, Olaf tried to make a living off the land. Over time, Olaf tried everything. Plants didn't grow well, the land seemed too barren to raise livestock. Olaf continued to curse his fathers stupidity when the landowner right next door had the good fortune of having water on his land. Olaf longed for the day he would have a well for water on his own land.

One day a German immigrant named Heinrich came to town. Heinrich said he was a well driller and could find water anywhere. Olaf gladly sold his 150 acres of land to Heinrich for $500.00. A tidy sum thought Olaf. Heinrich went about drilling for water, but always came up short. If ever he did manage to hit a spot of moisture, the water was cloudy or looked dirty. Over time, even hard headed Heinrich gave up looking for water on this wasteland. In 1972, when Heinrich was over 70 years old, a big oil company discovered Heinrich's land was on top of the famed Williston oil basin and after the oil company drilled their first well, Heinrich started receiving oil royalties in excess of a million dollars per year!

As long as the owners treated the land as worthless, it was useless. Once the land took on the life of an oil well, it held untold riches for the land owner!

Quite a fascinating story to read. Is it a story of fact or purely someone's imagination? Olaf never knew what wealth he had, Heinrich didn't know oil from dirty water. Over time what appears to be a useless cause can often lead to wealth beyond belief. It takes persistence, positive effort, and the willingness to look for the good in life. Was Olaf sorry for his dissatisfaction with his land? Did Olaf feel he lost out by selling his inheritance? How would you feel if you were Olaf?

Chapter 10

SO SORRY

A successful person has the confidence to apologize.

Apologizing for your errors, especially those errors you make which hurt others is an important part of recognizing joy in life, as well as demonstrating self confidence.

Unfortunately too many people find it hard to say they are sorry. We all make mistakes. There are times when we all are self centered.

If you can admit you are wrong, say you are sorry. By doing so you will prove you are a person who values life and values the relationship you trespassed upon.

Parents, husbands, and wives, sometimes fall into the trap of believing saying sorry is unnecessary, because their family is based on love, and universal forgiveness. After all, why say you are sorry, when the person knows you love them?

Perhaps you were caught late at the office and as a result missed the opening night of your son's play. You can't bring that time back so you can make the play, but you can and should say you are sorry. Maybe you can do something he likes to show him you are sorry. So, you missed the first night. Make the second night! Tell him you are sorry you missed opening night, and tell him of your pride in his performance. Maybe you missed his opening night 20 years ago, try calling him today, say you are sorry, show remorse, and work out an event today for the two of you. Perhaps a professional theatrical performance is available for you both to attend. Buy the tickets and go!

How tragic it is when we can not even have the faith in ourselves to express to our loved ones we are sorry when we err.

One day Benjamin told me he thought my teasing was too much, the opportunity presented itself for me to say I was sorry, or his feelings could have been ignored. I apologized, despite the fact I felt nothing wrong had been said. As our discussion moved forward, we enjoyed a great learning experience together about the importance of saying you are sorry when appropriate. Many examples of our family were used to enhance the meaning and importance of the topic. Today, it is my belief that Benjamin has gained the right perspective about how and when to say he is sorry. A good portion of this positive character trait in Benjamin resulted in my willingness to say I was sorry, and not ignore his opinions.

Being full of sorrow for your past errors isn't going to give you a better life, but as you identify some of these errors, take some action to create a new experience which demonstrates you want to live a better life now!

You will find as you create new happier events which replace your previous error filled events, you will develop better relationships and you will become more thankful for your enjoyable life.

Should you be a parent, do not be afraid to say you are sorry to your children. In most circumstances, you will be glad you said you were sorry!

Chapter 11

SAY THANK YOU

Sincere appreciation is a gift with no cost, yet it has monumental value to both the person giving and the person receiving.

One can never say thank you enough, and it is never too late to say thank you.

Some people find it difficult to show appreciation to others, even if simply through a verbal message. By showing your appreciation to someone for something by saying thank you or demonstrating your appreciation by your actions, you can discover a sense of goodness in yourself, resulting in a happier life.

Perhaps your spouse brings you flowers or writes an unexpected love note. Saying thank you is certainly in order, but if you really want to let your spouse know you are thankful, try doing something special in return. Maybe your spouse likes to go out for an ice-cream treat, forget your perpetual diet, get something with an ice cream store logo, (a napkin works great), write an invitation for an ice cream treat on the item.

Try this out for your ice cream eating spouse: How about a date at the Dairy Queen tonight? By the way the flowers (note) are beautiful! Written on a Dairy Queen napkin, you picked up on your way home. This action is guaranteed to get a positive result.

It really doesn't matter what the gesture is, but showing appreciation goes a long, long way to building a great life for yourself as well as building a great life with others around you.

While in graduate school, a great friend of mine was Craig Hanner. We both enjoyed racquetball, going to parties, and shared a lot of fun times together.

We would go to parties, search out single girls, and frequently played very competitive games of racquetball against each other.

Craig lived with some undergraduates, and would frequently find a fun party for us to join. Despite my zany antics employed while meeting co-eds, Craig put up with me and seemed to enjoy going to parties together. Over the course of two years we met a lot of people, and experienced part of life which many of our classmates missed.

We never established (or attempted to) who was the stronger racquetball player, but we played dozens of spirited games. Nearly twenty years past our receiving our Masters degrees, I sent Craig an e-mail thanking him for his friendship and our games of racquetball. Was 20 years too long to wait to say thank you?

Craig responded back to me with a message which really helped brighten my day. It is never too late to say thank you. A thankful life is often filled with a lot of great living. Perhaps Craig didn't need my message of thanks, but by taking the simple action of sending him the message, our friendship and our happy memories were enhanced. There is no reason not to say thank you, and it is never too late.

Chapter 12

LOOKING FOR GOOD

Every cloud has a silver lining.

Most of us have been told at one time or another "if you look hard enough, you can find the good in anything." This is probably true. But in reality, if you just look at anything with the right perspective, you can quickly see some good. You don't have to fight, sweat and toil to find some good in a person, situation or experience.

A rain storm unexpectedly erupts. A mother stands at the window and sees mud puddles. Her son sees the joy of splashing his way to school. How we respond to an unexpected rain storm is an important manifestation of our inner joy. Are you upset with or fascinated by the natural cleansing of the land by the rain? Learn to become fascinated with the greening of the grass. The natural cleaning of the streets and the joyous sounds of thunder.

The attitude we take towards rain storms, snow storms and the like can be positive. Just look a little and you will develop a good attitude towards the storms of life.

Storms in life are not only limited to rain, snow or hail, but personal tragedies, accidents and illness can be viewed as a storm to weather or as a permanent loss of joy. You will find life much more enjoyable if you weather the storms instead of living a life filled with catastrophes.

Chapter 13

PHYSICAL

Real strength is measured by the commitments you keep, not the pounds you can lift.

We are all endowed with different physical attributes. You can like your body or feel trapped by your body. We all are unique and we need to revel in our uniqueness. Short of plastic surgery you are stuck with what you got. Diet and exercise can make some good changes. But your attitude about yourself means the most. As your hair gets gray, become amazed with your changing body. If you frown too much, start smiling. Wear a smile and people around you will wonder why you are so lucky.

Laugh and people will laugh with you. It is said laughter is music to our souls, so why not play some music for your soul everyday? You may be thinking that's easy for him to say, but you should be thinking, it's possible for me to do. So start laughing and smiling today!

Accidents in life take a toll on all of us. Some accidents result in much pain and suffering. After a bad accident or illness you must choose how to respond.

In our community lives Judy Siegle. She is a very bright woman. She works at MeritCare Hospital and has had to overcome a major physical battle in her life.

Judy was a shining basketball player, who was named a Minnesota All-State player in high school. After high school, she planned for a great basketball career at Concordia College in Moorhead, Minnesota. The summer after high school, prior to starting college, she was involved in a terrible automobile accident. The accident left her a quadriplegic, initially paralyzed from the shoulders down.

Judy is not the kind of person to wait for life to find her, she embraces life each day. She faced horrible odds. How could she overcome such a tragedy for a spirited athlete?

Judy went to work on herself. She fought for a way to find a complete life. She fought so hard that she has become a world-class wheelchair Olympic athlete. In 1999, Judy won two gold medals in wheelchair racing at the Pan-Am games in Mexico City, Mexico, earning herself worldwide recognition for her accomplishment.

Today, Judy still makes physical exercise part of her life. Despite being classified as a quadriplegic, she has started to regain some muscle strength. Against every medical opinion she is moving herself forward.

Does every day take a lot of work for Judy? You bet it does. She constantly works herself physically, and must maintain an optimistic mental attitude to have a positive life in her wheelchair.

Judy continues to use her positive motivation with her mind to overcome her physical limitations.

Maybe you are not ever going to have a tragic accident like Judy. Could you face the odds? Could you put forth the effort necessary to beat the odds? You can, if you have the right mental attitude.

Your mental attitude can take on strength like Judy's did. You can take steps to grow your mind to become smarter and lead a more enjoyable life.

Chapter 14

YOUR MIND

A person who chooses not to read is no better than the person who can not read.

Much of your mental ability was pre-determined by your genetics at birth. Your education, attitude and environment have played a big part in how "smart" you are today as well as your genetics. Reading opens up a wonderful new world for anyone willing to pick up a book.

Most people consider Albert Einstein one of the smartest people to ever walk the earth. You can develop the "Einstein" attitude by believing in yourself. You will add much more to your life if you believe in your ability to learn.

Imagine for a moment you are standing in a baseball field, you look up to see an airplane racing through the sky. You, of course, know the airplane is moving because you are standing still on the ground as the airplane moves past you. You also see the plane moving past clouds. A beautiful sight isn't it?

Next imagine you are seated in that airplane, you look at the seat you are sitting in and unless the plane is shaking, the seat seems to be still, the seat doesn't appear to be moving does it?

Life is based on your experiences and perspective. It's all relative to how you choose to respond.

The airplane looked like it was moving because you were a distance away standing still on the ground. The airplane seat appeared to be stationary because you were sitting on it and the plane was not shaking.

If you think about this airplane example for a moment, you will surely recognize the seat was moving just as fast as the airplane, but the seat didn't seem to be moving based on your ability to see the seat and your perspective. Where you were relative to the airplane and the seat determined your perspective.

I hope this airplane example helps show you you can be as smart as you want. If you do feel you essentially grasp the concept of the airplane and the seat; congratulate yourself on being able to understand the premise of relative motion.

The premise of relative motion is not an easy concept to grasp unless you can read, can use your mind to visualize, use your past experiences seeing an airplane and traveling on an airplane. Our minds are wonderful tools designed for a lifetime of enjoyment. Include in your life the personal perspective you can learn, understand and be a smart person. Such a positive perspective will add a lot of joy to your life.

Growing your mind not only helps you, but can help you enhance your relationships with others.

Think about the airplane example. You can understand it, and you know you are smart.

Unfortunately we tend to measure how "smart" we are by the answers we have to questions we receive. A person my have all the right answers, but still be as ignorant as a rock.

You can read every poem ever written, you may even memorize some. That information about poetry still doesn't make you a poet.

A person may study the design of cabinets, know every type of wood, know every type of joint, nail, glue, glide, hardware, etc. This person may even take a test to show how much he knows, but all this information doesn't enable him to build a simple cabinet. The person needs to build to be a carpenter, not have the right answers on a test.

Similarly one can study the bible and learn everything about God and Jesus, but that doesn't mean the person knows God or uses this information in a way to enhance relationships according to Gods word.

You can study every book available about how to ride a bicycle. A person can only learn to ride a bike when they get on a bicycle, attempt to ride, fall a few times, and finally succeed.

Real knowledge is the application of information in useful ways. A dictionary is useless information until it is used to enhance your vocabulary or enhance your understanding of a words meaning.

Chapter 15

RELATIONSHIPS

*Every friendship maintained is more valuable than a
newly minted gold coin.*

We are a social animal, we live amongst others
like us and others very different from us. Once
again, our personal perspective and how we use
our mind can determine how well we live. Do you
look for the positive good in others, or are you
quick to condemn?

Arriving home from MeritCare Hospital required
me to be in a wheel chair. Concern grew that
people would not respond well to me in a wheel
chair; obviously disabled. Our local school system
follows an open integration philosophy and most
children have classmates in wheel chairs starting
with kindergarten.

When Dad came home in a wheelchair he was
viewed as normal by Benjamin and Caleb, just
like anybody else. Our children had learned
through their experiences in the Fargo public
schools, people in wheel chairs were not an
oddity. My welcoming home was made much
easier by my children's immediate acceptance of
my wheel chair. Some adult friends had a hard
time relating to me in a wheel chair. The
relationships between myself and our children
grew from my disability. Fortunately my children
have a good perspective about people in wheel
chairs.

One of the greatest rewards of our family wheel chair experience came when our son Caleb chose to help his disabled wheel-chair confined classmate during his class play in second grade. He saw his friend in need of help. She was simply a friend in need. He viewed her as perfectly normal. She was not odd or someone to be hesitant to interact with. He liked her, so he helped her. Needless to say, we were very proud of Caleb for his actions that day, and as a result gained greater joy in our lives.

My father never played baseball with me, so naturally I wanted to teach my children how to play. My son Benjamin was perfectly happy to play catch with me while my life was confined to a wheel-chair. He gave me encouragement and helped me to develop a positive attitude about the possibility of eliminating the need for a wheel-chair. Once again, his school experience provided him with the right perspective about life. Benjamin demonstrated his unconditional love to me by playing with me in spite of the wheel chair. Today we play catch as often as we can, and we make it a point to go to all his Babe-Ruth baseball games together.

As we see new places and interact with new people, we can grow to learn more about our world. With the right attitude traveling our world can be a great part of living. Should a person have a different language, different skin color, be in a wheel chair or whatever, we need to accept them as they are.

We need to learn people are people and learn to live without classifications. All human relationships can be better if we accept one another.

Poland, Russia, Canada, America are all different countries. Does it really matter where you were born? Should your birthplace determine if you are an acceptable person? We all need to accept each other as one common group of people.

Pride in your heritage is a good thing, but we should not arbitrarily classify people based on their heritage. If you feel a sense of pride in your heritage, work to earn yourself a trip to your forefathers homeland.

Chapter 16

GO TRAVELING

The bigger your world the bigger you will be as a person.

When expanding our boundaries by traveling through the world, we can use these experiences to enhance our lives, or become fearful of the world. We set mental boundaries for our zone of travel comfort.

An infant is bound by the area she is allowed to explore by her parents. We set distance from home boundaries for our young children. What most of us don't realize is we set the same boundaries for ourselves as adults.

At one time in history it was not unusual for people to never leave the city where they were born, or never pass the borders of their state. As we expanded our boundaries as a group, we became more enlightened. Our lives became richer and we greatly enhanced our lives. Risk of harm is a concern as we travel to new places. Today, all of us can make our lives much more enjoyable by exploring past our self imposed boundaries. Can anyone today even begin to grasp the curiosity Marco Polo must have contained to explore new lands? Think of how thrilled he must have been to uncover unknown people, places and things. You can be a modern day Marco Polo in your own world. Take a walk through a museum or art gallery.

Change to a different grocery store. If you are like most people, you have picked one grocery store, and do most of your shopping there because it is within your self determined zone of comfort. Take a small step forward and try out a new grocery store!

Even something as simple as going to a different grocery store can bring more to your life, if you take the time to explore. Believe it or not, a new grocery store can give you the same experience as traveling to a different country. Simple things like this can greatly enhance your life and help develop an appreciation for living within you.

All new things you experience are created through your state of mind.

Should you choose to physically transport yourself through planes, trains or automobiles, you will discover much enjoyment. You should explore the world.

You do not need to actually physically travel to experience the world. By reading, you can travel anywhere your mind is willing to go. Videos to rent or own are available for your enjoyment. Pick up a few travel videos, watch them to expand your understanding of the world. Perhaps one or two cultures will make you very curious. If so, supplement your videos with a few good books to read about this culture which intrigues you.

Chapter 17

READ

True knowledge is the application of information.

If you want to live a better life, the best advise you can accept is simply to read. Reading can take you anywhere you want to go. Through your imagination, with the help of a good book or two you can see the ocean floors, experience outer space, talk to your hero, believe in the continent of Atlantis, or anything else you want to learn about.

Reading is a perfect way to expand your life. Reading is a great way to experience more out of life. Our public libraries contain volumes of material available on just about any subject you wish to learn about. We have already demonstrated you have a great mind, so expand your mind by reading a few different books! Remember the Einstein within you.

If you have a pet hamster you probably would never consider taking this hamster to a veterinarian which was known to have stopped reading about animals when he graduated from school. There is never a time to stop learning in life. One of the ingredients of a successful, enjoyable life is a lifetime of learning! Read, read, read!

Chapter 18

IMAGINATION

As necessity is said to be the mother of invention,
desire is the mother of success.

We all have imaginations. Some of us develop strong imaginations to help us enjoy life. Some of us use our imaginations to inflict pain upon our lives.

A great way to move towards a happier life is simply by imagining you have the attributes of life which are important to you. Imagine yourself as happy not sad. Take actions you imagine to make yourself happy.

Should you wish to have a better relationship with your co-workers, use your imagination to visualize them congratulating you for a job well done. Use your imagination to visualize you sharing positive experiences. Should you do these two simple things with your imagination, you will discover the people you work with get better and better. Use your imagination towards your fellow employees in negative ways and you will damage your opinion of your co-workers.

Of course how you use your imagination with personal work relations is only one way to improve your life. How about your spouse, your kids?

Playing with one of my best friends growing up we often ended in some sort of trouble. As an adult it baffles me how we could get in one kind of trouble after another. We both thought our parents must have believed we were bad kids. His mother once related to me how she viewed us. She simply stated "you two were very mischievous little boys". What a great attitude to view our trouble as mischief, no wonder she tolerated our endless pranks and problems.

While discussing our mischievous childhood I said to this mother of my friend, "If you ever wondered if we did something but never found out for sure, you should assume we didn't do it, because we always got caught!"

Fortunately we did get caught at almost every wrong thing we did. Had we not been caught and taught right from wrong, we could have easily moved to more significant trouble as we aged. Our parents cared enough to teach us right from wrong, yet despite the fear of punishment, we were constantly pushing our boundaries, most often ending in trouble.

Your perspective and how you use your imagination do have a big impact on your life.

Chapter 19

MAKE AN IMPACT

It has been said that Abraham Lincoln's mother told him "be somebody Abe." Most everyone would agree Abraham Lincoln did indeed become someone. Abe made a choice in his life to make an impact on the lives of others. What ever he became involved with he worked, studied and demanded excellence.

We all are faced with the same choice as Abraham Lincoln to make an impact or not. Long after you're gone from this world what you do today will be remembered or forgotten based on the impact you had on your fellow man.

Should you determine that your mission is to create life long memories for your children, you can arrange for special times together like decorating the house together for Halloween, trick or treating the neighborhood on Halloween each year, or spending the Fourth of July together as a family. Positive memories like these can be created with minimal effort.

Our Thanksgivings and Easter holiday meals usually included my mothers two brothers, Clark and Jon, as well as their families. My mother would cook a feast for us all, and as a result of sharing these holidays, we became a fairly close group.

My mother's brother Clark lived on a lake in Minnesota until he moved in the 1970's. We often drove to Uncle Clarks for added family time. The drive seemed torture to me. Clark always had a fishing boat for us to use, something new for us to experience, and a warm heart. Today the memories of growing up with my cousins is a positive way to remember life as a kid. Maybe the long drive was unnecessary; perhaps we don't need our relatives, but the experiences as a child definitely enhanced my life.

Clark's son Brian and I were close in age. We remain good friends today. When it was time for my two boys to test their luck at fishing, Brian willingly agreed to use his boat and make the event possible. We traveled to Brian's childhood home on the lake to fish. We shared stories of our time together fishing, swimming, and learning about life.

Brian knew just where to go to find fish. Benjamin and Caleb had a terrific time on their first fishing trip. Reliving the sound of Benjamin exclaiming "Look, Dad, I caught a fish!" has a positive impact on my attitude. Hearing both Caleb and Benjamin talk about what great fishermen they are also is very heartwarming.

Long after Clark, Brian and I are gone, our presence will shine in the memories of Benjamin and Caleb. As these two boys share their story of their first fishing expedition, it is very likely Brian, myself and Brian's father Clark will become immortal. Our lives will live on because we all chose to have a strong positive impact on the lives of others. The choices we make everyday can have an impact which lasts long past our lifetimes.

One night Brian and his wife invited us out to their home for dinner. It was the first time Berea had joined the boys for an outing without her mom. Berea had an absolutely wonderful time, and this outing was a definite turning point in the relationship between Berea and myself. Because of Brian and his wife's willingness to share their home, my life received the great rewards of getting to know my daughter better. We laughed, talked, and generally just had a terrific time. This simple evening will be a lifetime memory for all of us.

Chapter 20

LIVING FOREVER

A hero is remembered, a legend lives forever.

People come and go every day. New people are born, grow old, and eventually die. We all carry memories of the people whom have had an impact on our lives. Those people we truly loved, cared about, and experienced life with, never leave us.

Think for a moment about someone you really loved who has passed on. As vividly as possible imagine them, perhaps even speak a word or two listening for the answer they would give you.

If you do this exercise with your whole heart, you will discover the spirit of this loved one is alive and still very much with you.

This exercise is not to be interpreted as some sort of attempt at magic or to try to conjure up spirits in the sense of witchcraft or trickery. Crystal balls, drawing out spirits of the dead is not reality.

Reality is what you feel in your heart. A real sprit is the love and memories you carry with you.

Should you choose to create positive experiences and have an impact on those you love, you can live forever! Life is for living and the more you choose to excel at living with those you love, the longer you can live in their hearts.

Chapter 21

24 HOURS A DAY

Time is the one asset we all can choose to use or waste.

Should we be blessed with a full day of life we receive 24 hours, which is 1,440 minutes or 86,400 seconds each day. Why is it some people get so much more out of these 24 hours than others? Do you embrace life or choose to watch the days go by? Life is meant for participation, it is not a spectator event.

The choices you make during each of the 86,400 seconds in each day determines how much you live that day. If you choose to hug each member of your family you choose to receive hugs back, those hugs will enhance your life.

Part of my personal commitment to my family is to simply tell each person in my family "I love you," everyday. It may seem like a small thing, but it takes at least some effort to say I love you, and sometimes during or after an argument the words can be hard to find. But even if it takes fifteen seconds per person, that's only one minute of my day. One minute per day to insure we acknowledge love per person is very little compared to the loss felt if even one member of our family ever wondered if love was part of our lives.

Studies have proven that married couples who take the time to embrace and share a real kiss each day will experience happier marriages, live longer and be more prosperous. Are you willing to choose to take such a simple action to insure more happiness, prosperity and more life? Are you too busy to stop your life to embrace your spouse? If you think you are too busy to share a short embrace or have more important things to do, You are a fool. By not having the willingness to even take this simple step you are consciously choosing to forfeit some pleasures in your life.

It is amazing when the more we know we have to accomplish in a given day, the more we can get done. It often seems the more we must do the more we do, but in setting our sights on accomplishment too many of us pass up opportunities to enhance how we live. We become too busy to tell those we love how we love them, let alone take the time to demonstrate our love.

Living a full life involves paying attention to every aspect of life. A full life will bring much more enjoyment to you and your loved ones, but living life to its fullest takes effort to identify and pursue what living life means to you.

It is worth the effort to identify your desires and create the right balance for your own life.

Chapter 22

LIFE'S BALANCE
Walking a tight rope is a challenge, falling from a tight rope is a disaster.

In one way or another, everyone works for the right balance for living an enjoyable life as they define it. Each person chooses to pursue their balance based on their individual desires, wants and needs. No two people view life the same. Each person is motivated in different ways.

In most cases, a drug addict is a highly motivated individual. We can see this motivation through the addict's constant desire to achieve another fix or acquire more of the item of their addiction. Nothing can stand in the way of an addict. Many addicts loose sight of reality and morality to feed their addiction. Addiction creates bad motivation resulting in bad actions.

An intelligent individual will assess life to discover their personal desires and through this process create a balanced life for themselves.

A positively balanced life only occurs by purpose. You determine what is important in your life. By consciously seeking a balance, we are able to guide ourselves to a more fulfilling existence. Your thoughts, actions, and desires will propel you to that which you value most. Make your desires good, positive, productive. This will usually create a life where your actions match those good positive productive desires. A great life does require finding your own balance to living.

Chapter 23

BALANCE CHALLENGE

On the following page is a chart designed to help you establish where you are in regards to some of the various aspects of life which are important. By using this chart, you can determine where you are in your life based on your standards. You should use it to determine what areas in your life you wish to enhance. You should use it as the starting point to guide you towards effective goal setting for your life.

How to use the balance challenge:

You should begin by rating yourself today based on your level of satisfaction in each aspect of your life today. Use a scoring system of 1 to 10 with one being not so good, and 10 being perfect. Or, if you prefer use grade scaling of A, B, C, D, E, and F.

Your current direction score is very important to this exercise. Recently have you been improving in this aspect of your life or is it getting worse?? Judge for yourself. Do you like your direction? What matters is how you feel, not how others think you should be. Most of the time you probably want to be getting better or improving. Although, sometimes getting worse is the right direction for your life.

Life Aspect	Todays Score	Your Current Direction ↓ or ↑	Your Long Term Desired Score	Action you can take to move you closer to your Desired Score
Physical				
Mental				
Financial				
Career				
Community				
Faith/Hope				
Religion				
Stress				
Attitude				
Spiritual				
Thankfulness				
Honesty				
Ethics/Integrity				
Teaching				
Relationships				
- Spouse				
- Children				
- Parents				
- Friends				
Stress				
Daily Motivation Level				
Your Over-all Self Rating				

Perhaps you have determined you are spending too much time with friends at the expense of your family, so consciously you are de-emphasizing this aspect of your life, so it is going down in direction. Do you really want everything going up at once? Is it reasonable to assume your life could be rebalanced so every aspect was going the same direction at the same time? Over a number of years of work everything can get better for you. Sometimes you need to make trade-offs.

Your long term desired score is critical to establishing your goals and setting your direction in life.

All 10's is not reasonable unless you are superman or superwoman. You need to assess where you really want to expend your efforts.

Perhaps you want a perfect career, and a perfect relationship with your spouse. By taking action to achieve these perfect states in your life, you can expect you may fall short somewhere else, perhaps you will loose ground either mentally or physically. Maybe a 5, 6, or 7 on each of mental and physical is your long term desired score. You decide what you want. Your score is what you need to focus on. Only you can determine what you truly want.

The object is to achieve the level of life enjoyment which you desire. By finding and achieving the right score in each area for your life you will find daily direction and maintain your personal motivation towards fulfillment during your entire life.

Chapter 24

COMMITMENT

We are measured by those things which we accomplish, not by the things we say we are going to do.

If you truly want to build an exceptional life for yourself become a person of commitment. Always follow through with any and every thing you say you intend to do.

Should your life be filled with unfulfilled promises and many going-to-do's, you fill your days with unnecessary clutter. With many items left undone you will tend to loose focus on what is important to you. If you suggest a lunch date to a friend, set a date, time and place, then be there on time!

Constantly making well intentioned suggestions will get you no where. If you really mean what you say you will do whatever you say you will.

Promises are worthless without a commitment to make the promise come true.

Often when a person is placed in a position of responsibility with an employer, the new manager has many ideas. Often a new manager will suggest to employees a bright future or possibilities of financial rewards. These well intentioned suggestions lead to disaster over time. You should always be able to put in writing your promises or plans if you are committed to them.

Should you be placed in a position of authority, it is even more important for you to follow through with your employ conversations in writing. If you can't write it out for the person you don't have the authority or you are not sincere.

Employees should expect every employer to provide them a commitment to their future. Should an employee be given an opportunity for advancement it should be clearly spelled out. Expecting full commitment between an employee and employer should be the way every business is run.

Commitment is a two way street. The sooner you live your life as a commitment to your life the sooner you will discover your life contains more enjoyment.

We like to play a lot of golf. We typically play a rather strict game. Benjamin watches his score very closely. He plays with no mulligans (do over shots), and is very competitive. Most golfers take a mulligan once in awhile. When golfing with a serious group occasionally it can add a lot to a game to create some laughter. Some serious golfers take this laughter to mean a person lacks commitment to the game.

If you find yourself golfing with a group that seems too determined to win, try suggesting a few "gimmie" puts, sometimes outrageous gimmies. If anyone in this responds with frustration, try this response: "Learn to enjoy life, if anyone of us thinks we are going to earn our living by golfing, we better get used to being mighty hungry!" When a ball finds its way into a water hazard, counting the skips and proclaiming a new skipping record can add some fun to a game. Usually everyone gets the point of this attempted levity. As long as everyone is treated equitably, no one gets hurt, the game is a game. The point is not to encourage cheating, but to have more fun together. After all, we play to enjoy ourselves.

Adding an element of fun, or some laughter to a game doesn't necessarily mean a person lacks commitment to excellence, but a reckless abandonment of the rules of a game is not the right way to go about life. We all live by some general rules and living within these rules will help you enjoy life. As a golfer, a great score will mean a lot more with no mulligans. The real key is learning to enjoy whatever you do.

If you are finding activities in your life are just not interesting or not very enjoyable anymore, you have a bad attitude, and you can be sure your bad attitude is negatively affecting others around you. You can change your attitude to enhance your enjoyment, and by changing yourself you will be amazed at how much better others around you are, and as a consequence you will enjoy more of your life.

Chapter 25

ENJOY LIFE

Pleasure is what you get from something, happiness is how you feel.

Each of us experience different levels of enjoyment from our lives. Each of us enjoys different things.

You must determine what you enjoy most in your life and pursue what you enjoy.

Perhaps you love to read while your spouse loves to watch football on Television. These are very compatible goals. You set aside the "game-time" to go to the library. Both of you can derive enjoyment from these activities. What if spending time together with your spouse is more important to you than reading? Try getting tickets for both of you to a game. By acquiring the game tickets you will show commitment to your marriage, and you have a much better chance of finding a more enjoyable time together. If tickets to a game are not feasible, suggest you would like to snuggle up with your spouse and read a book during the next game. These two simple choices could change your marriage!

Many marriages, including my own, suffer when during the courtship process both people enjoy activities together, but one person decides after marriage such activities were not all that enjoyable or the activities are no longer important to them for a full life.

Everyone has known someone who fell into this pre-marital trap: The "Honey, I love to (hunt, golf, fish, travel, visit your parents, etc.)", and so the marriage is consummated with the expectation the activities would continue. But, then one day you got married, and surprise! Your parents are too boring (golf is no fun, travel is too tiresome, fishing stinks, etc., etc.).

Just because your likes and dislikes are different from someone else's does not make either of you right or wrong. The right answer is to discover things you enjoy together. Be honest, changing without warning is bound to create stress in your marriage and family.

My son Caleb loves to ride his bike and roller blade. He especially likes to go over jumps on both his bike and his roller blades. He also enjoys the game of chess. His brother Benjamin, on the other hand, loves chess, likes to ride bike and roller blade but chooses not to jump his bike very often.

Caleb thinks he has a lot more fun on his bike than his brother. Benjamin sees his brother crash and thinks his brother is foolish. Benjamin is proud to be a winner at chess, while Caleb chooses not to be upset if he looses a game.

Both of these children are very special and each is unique. Each gets a great amount from life every day. Both enjoy their lives very much, yet in very different ways.

If you have children or have siblings, you probably recognize differences are a good thing. Part of our maturing as individuals involves accepting life's differences.

As a father, if a trick bike, a jump, or a special chess set are purchased but left unused without explanation, it can be very frustrating. As with anything one chooses to pursue in life, one must make the commitment to learn and grow or a great deal of life will pass you by.

Should it be a change in attitude about relatives, golf, fishing, travel, bicycling, chess or what have you. A great life filled with enjoyment also involves learning to change and accepting change in others around you. If your marriage was consummated with the expectation of support in certain activities, be sure you keep your commitment and do what you said you would. Otherwise you are asking for trouble with your spouse. If you always keep your commitments, you will find great joy in knowing you are an extraordinary person.

If that one time magical activity with your spouse fades in importance, work together to discover something new, but equally as magical. Grow together with this new found experience to gain some magic in your life.

Chapter 26

YOUR ELEVENTH COMMANDMENT

Thou shalt have no other gods before me.

Thou shalt not make unto thee any graven image, or any likeness of any thing that is in heaven above, or that is in the earth beneath, or that is in the water under the earth.

Thou shalt not take the name of the LORD thy God in vain; for the LORD will not hold him guiltless that taketh his name in vain.

Remember the Sabbath day, to keep it holy.

Honour thy father and thy mother: that thy days may be long upon the land which the LORD thy God giveth thee.

Thou shalt not kill.

Thou shalt not commit adultery.

Thou shalt not steal.

Thou shalt not bear false witness against thy neighbor.

Thou shalt not covet thy neighbour's house, thou shalt not covet they neighbour's wife, nor his manservant, nor his maidservant, nor his ox, nor his ass, nor any thing that is thy neighbour's.

God chose to give us ten pure rules to guide our lives. Should you choose to explore the bible more fully, you will discover these ten rules have a lot deeper meaning. Through the various stories of the bible, you will discover a number of ways to enhance your life by expanding Gods commandments to include what you learn from His teachings. You should follow the ten commandments, and you must determine additional rules for living your life based on what you believe God wants you to do.

In reality, we all pick some rules which we use to guide our lives, but we far too often allow negative circumstances or negative events to harden our outlook which results in our not experiencing the joy of life which God intended for each of us.

If you are finding certain relationships in your life have turned for the worse, it is probably very likely due to your unwillingness to look both at your past actions and to look to the future. You may not be recognizing how you have chosen to sabotage your own success. For most of us it is easier to blame the other guy for our own errors.

We often face unexpected challenges in life. How you respond to life when you find yourself at a fork in the road will be determined by your attitude and how well balanced your life is at the time.

Sometimes it is good to let your frustrations show. As most golfers will attest, a person can line up a put, visualize a perfect hit, have everything set-up and still miss the cup by a wide margin. At the time of the miss-hit, some golfers rant and rave, making a fool out of themselves. Others just shrug off the miss as if it didn't matter. Somewhere in the middle of these two approaches is probably best. You don't want to make a fool of yourself over a golf shot, but you can make an exclamation of your disappointment without offending anyone. Neither keeping all your frustrations inside or letting all your frustrations out (explosively) will serve your best interests in life.

If you find yourself consistently getting bad results in relationships, you are most likely approaching issues in ways which lead to your bad results. You need to change your approach. To think you can get different results from doing the same thing over and over is crazy. To change a desired outcome, you must change your approach.

We all seek to find a balance to our world which fits into our expectations and life rules. A life without some rules will end up out of balance. We need to learn how to accept changes to create a new balance once change occurs.

It is up to you to figure out a way to express yourself appropriately. Maybe, to further the golf put example, you say out loud, something like, fiddlesticks or Why is that ball crooked? Or look, my putter is bent? You can devise a number of responses to help you relax and at the same time acknowledge your frustration. Not only should you devise responses for poor golf shots, but you should devise them to use in all disappointing life events.

Chapter 27

LEARNING ACCEPTANCE

Freedom allows you a new life anytime you choose it.

All of us are different. All of us view life's experiences differently.

As we face great trials in our life such as illness or the death of a loved one, we go through various stages of grief, denial, and eventually acceptance. We don't really want to believe what has happened. As a man disabled by a stroke once said "I never dream I'm in a wheel chair."

Even though he knows his life is confined to a wheel chair, he doesn't fully accept it in his mind. Racial prejudice is caused by not being able to accept differences.

On the other hand, if a person accepts they are stuck where they are, the person is bound to be unhappy. Some things we just cannot change. For those we can't change, we need to learn acceptance.

Choosing to live a fully appreciative life should cause us to marvel at the difference between the colors of the flowers at the florist shop. We all need to accept and relish these same differences in other aspects of our world.

A major part of accepting others and being accepted yourself involves how sincere you are when you communicate the differences in your life to others around you.

Part of learning acceptance involves understanding that you can change. If you have been hurt in some way you need to accept the hurt in the past, but learn from the past and change your ways so you don't get hurt again!

Chapter 28

LEARN TO CHANGE

You can only change by changing your attitude.

As long as you keep doing things the way you have always done them, you are probably going to keep getting the same results you have been getting. None of us can change the past, but any one of us can change our future by what we do.

Alfred was a man who became financially rich many times in his life by being a trend spotting genius. Alfred seemed to always spot a big trend before anyone else. Once he spotted this new trend he would sell everything he owned and invest in this new trend. He would ride the trend to the top, become very rich, hold on until finally the trend ended and he lost everything. Time after time, Alfred's life followed this same pattern. He spotted the changes society was making far before anyone else, but he never learned to change his approach and as a result he died broke.

Are you at the forefront of change, or do you only change when you are forced to? Learning to change takes conscious effort.

The Balance Challenge covered earlier is designed to help you identify what you want to change in your life, so use it.

Change is simple. First, identify what you want in your life (or what results you are getting you don't like). Second, accept that you need to make some changes yourself to get what you do want. Third, identify what you can do to change to get these desired results to occur. When you start to realize what you want from your life, you will make changes much more easily.

Some days we all look for more material possessions for our enjoyment, but most of us do have the money we need to lead an enjoyable life each day without extra possessions. Perhaps not every day is our idea of a perfect day, but certainly we have the potential of daily enjoyment without millions of dollars in the bank.

Chapter 29

BIG DEAL

If you show you care, others around you will care for you.

To create a positive life experience every day one must put meaning on every moment of time. How often have you responded to an event by saying "its no big deal, who cares anyway!" Perhaps at the time this seemingly small event in your life appeared to be unimportant. Over time, many of these unimportant events will add up to some real significance in your life. If you consider yourself an individualist, materialist or spiritualist, every event has some meaning.

Learning to live in the moment is fun and can be an exciting way to live. We must determine for ourselves what holds importance. You must pay attention to the important events of life and learn to let the unimportant events go.

It may seem to be no big deal if you fail to tell your daughter you love her one day. But one day often turns into two days, then three days, then a year, then years turn into a lifetime. Only a fool would consider a lifetime of not telling their daughter she was loved to be no big deal. Be it your daughter, your son, your wife, your husband, your mother, father, whomever. You are smart to let those you love know how you love them before they are gone from this world, or you loose them to someone else.

Think it is no big deal if you don't desire the touch of your wife (husband)? You best think again before you discover someone else touching her (him) in ways you don't want someone else doing any touching!

Chapter 30

THE INDIVIDUALISTS

I may be the most important to me, yet I is the smallest word we know.

For the individualist, every event should have an impact on their life. So your son spilled the orange juice. No big deal, right? If you want to use the spilled juice to grow yourself and your son as individuals you should view this as a learning event for both of you.

Don't yell at your son for this small error. Don't say to your son, who cares about the juice – it's no big deal. Rather than brushing the spilled juice off as unimportant, the individualist will use the next few moments to teach important life lessons. Someone who loves their son and desires to share a love for life with their son will not scream or yell at spilled juice.

The true individualist will calmly explain to her son how her son's actions could have been altered so the juice wasn't spilled. The individualist will then make sure her son cleans up the mess.

Once the juice mess is cleaned up, the individualist who loves her son will explain the juice spill caused certain consequences like a delay in leaving home, no juice for breakfast, or extra wasted time spent cleaning up the mess, etc.

A good natured, loving individualist will not yell or punish her son for a simple accident. An individualist will use events of life to help create more appreciation and better understanding of the consequences for actions one takes in life. Individualists can create negative attitudes or build positive, learning life experiences for themselves and those they love.

An individualist does not have to be a person who thinks she has done it all by herself. A positive individualist takes in the events of life in an appreciative way, learning from each event how to be a better person.

You should work to learn to appreciate life if you are inclined to be more of an individualist. Use the daily events of life to become more satisfied with what you have. The individualist will frequently search to determine how her life can become better.

As the saying goes, you should not cry over spilled milk. Milk spilled like orange juice is not a significant loss, but it is an opportunity to teach a life lesson. The material value is not important to a positive individualist.

Chapter 31

THE MATERIALIST

Broken wheels can be fixed, broken hearts have to heal.

There is little doubt materialism in our current society is looked down upon. A materialist is not a bad person, nor is a materialist creating less good for our world than a non-material orientated person.

As a materialist, you need to seek out ways in which you can use your predisposition to worldly goods to enhance your life experiences and the experiences of those around you.

Most materialists want to get right to the heart of the matter, or get right to the bottom line.

The fact of the matter is, like it or not, without materialists we would have worse schools, much worse health care provided, and a much lower standard of living.

As a materialist, you can grow your appreciation for the finer things in life. If you find the idea of a bright colored cotton shirt more appealing than a polyester blend, then work to acquire the shirt of your choice, when you wear it take a couple of seconds to pay particular attention to how good this pure cotton shirt makes you feel. Enjoy the moments to their highest. Recognize you are

86

bathing yourself in natures cotton, made especially for you and for your enjoyment. Maybe this orientation strikes you as being non-Godly, but if your disposition is toward materialism, use this to better appreciate Gods natural gifts to us; like cotton. Use your materialistic tendencies to build a better world for all of society, not just to gather more things to use for yourself.

Strongly desiring material possessions is not in and of itself bad. What is most important is how you deal with your material possessions.

One year for his birthday, Benjamin received ten coins from his Grandma Marcia. Using this as a teaching opportunity, we separated the coins and he distributed them as follows;

> 1 coin to the church (10%)
>
> 1 coin to a person in need (10%)
>
> 1 coin to his brother (10%)
>
> 1 coin to his sister (10%)
>
> 4 coins to his savings account (40%)
>
> 2 coins spent on candy (20%)

We felt this was the proper way to teach him how to tend to his financial wealth for life. He received joy from each coin and from each decision on each coins use.

Even the most fanatical materialist can create good in a way acceptable to the most fanatical spiritualist.

Chapter 32

THE SPIRITUALIST

Blue skies are as much an attitude as they are an act of nature.

The spiritualist looks at life as a gift from God, believing all good things come to us through his divine nature.

To believe God plays a part in the good of your life can have a tremendously positive impact on your appreciation for life.

Take a moment right now to take a deep breath. If you consider the air you breathe and the smells which you notice in the air are put there for you by God, you can have a spiritually enriching experience. If you want to think the air is no big deal, hold your breath for 45 seconds! Which is a more enjoyable experience?

As you look about this world, finding splendor and joy in the songs of the birds can ad a great deal to your day. Of course, your attitude determines how you respond to the birds awakening you at five o'clock in the morning. A good strong spiritualist will wake to the birds songs with prayers of thanksgiving for another day of life and prayers of happiness for the gift of the birds songs.

Spending hours in prayer or learning all the right answers from the Bible does not mean you will grow to appreciate and know God. Having the right answers means nothing. The true spiritualist demonstrates his or her oneness with God through daily actions.

The tremendous controversy with child abuse by catholic priests in early 2002 clearly demonstrates how one can claim to have the right answers but not follow the teachings as the teachings were meant to be followed.

We all know someone who claims to be a spiritualist but acts more satanic when no one is watching. Equally we all know someone who demonstrates life skills and a compassion which glorifies God, when the person doesn't claim to be a true believer.

Cynthia's grandfather Marcel never openly acknowledged his belief in God, claimed no strong church affiliation, and rarely attended church, yet, everyday through his actions and praise of his wonderful, but modest life, he lived as a great example to those around him. Whenever Cynthia would talk of her fear that her grandfather didn't believe in God, my response was always to point out how he lived his life. God is going to judge us by what we do in life, not just what we say. Never has anyone questioned if Marcel is in heaven now. He lived by example not words. His example showed a deep spiritual acceptance.

If you want to be a real spiritualist or believe you are, you must take action to demonstrate your beliefs by how you treat those you love, how you respond to evil, and how much gratitude you have for the many great gifts God has given us to enjoy in this world.

How our relationship develops with our God, only we can determine. Appreciating the gifts of nature will help you find a stronger sense of spirituality.

Chapter 33

I.M.S.

You and I together make us.

Thus far, you have probably identified yourself as having the tendencies of an individualist, a materialist or a spiritualist. What your current disposition is can be changed to better fit what you think is right. There is no one right way for everyone, only one right way for you.

A great way to live life more fully is to understand that all aspects of life can provide you some level of enjoyment. Create a mixture of the individualist, the materialist, and the spiritualist within yourself. Find the beauty in the wonderful gift of a particular item God created for your life and relish it, take it in with all your senses, how it feels, how it smells, how it tastes, how it sounds. Use this one fantastic item in your life as your learning point for appreciating everything around you.

The experience Cynthia and I had of seeing the Bald Eagle in Wisconsin is a good example of strengthening life by using the approach to believing the Eagle was put there simply for our personal enjoyment. The materialist was evident in the fact we were in a man-made aluminum canoe. Without the canoe, we would have missed the experience. The spiritualist was involved as we both viewed the Eagle as one of Gods great creations for all to enjoy. All of our senses were stimulated and we still feel the power of this great experience today through our memories.

We have an exceptional sideboard (piece of wood furniture) in our home which is one of my symbols of a thankful life. The wood is exquisite, the craftsmanship exceptional. This particular piece of furniture appeals to my every sense. Esthetically, it looks terrific, it is a piece which is mine, it is a beautiful creation inspired by man but allowed by Gods gift of nature. For my life this sideboard creates joy for the individualist within me, is certainly a material possession, and transcends to a strong feeling of spirituality.

Picture yourself on a sunny beach. To get to the beach you needed transportation (a material item). You can take in the sounds, smells and feel the sun and believe its all yours (the individualist). You can say a good positive prayer of thanksgiving for all the gifts and all your stimulated senses (the spiritualist). Just using your imagination this way will lead to a more joyful life. Truly enjoying the real experience in this very purposeful way will give you a greater feeling of living life.

Once you begin to develop a greater appreciation of everything around you, you can better define and discover your true purpose for life.

Chapter 34

PLAY YOUR GAME

Everyone loves a winner; few cheer the looser after the game.

Life is meant for participation. Life is not a spectator sport. However, you need to define what your game is and how to play it for yourself.

When on the golf course, Benjamin and I play golf competitively and take our scores seriously. This type of golf is fun for us. We both think we should not get caught up on our scores, but our natural tendency is to work to achieve our best score every game.

Caleb finds playing golf too slow. After finding a few lost golf balls, Caleb decided finding lost balls was a lot more fun than hitting the little white things around the course. We bought him a ball retriever to use in water. We asked our club manager if Caleb could search for balls as long as he didn't disrupt other players. Upon getting our club managers approval, Caleb began playing his own game of search and find. One day he found over thirty golf balls. Each successive time out on the course he worked to exceed his best day of finding golf balls.

We decided Caleb would get paid ten dollars for one hundred golf balls. Within a short time, he had earned his first ten dollars, immediately he started towards his next hundred golf balls. This is a great example of someone adjusting a sport to become his own game. Caleb is thrilled to find lost golf balls, and is very excited with a ten dollar reward when he earns it.

At first, Benjamin and I tried to convince Caleb to play a normal game of golf, but as time passed, we realized Caleb had learned how to participate in golf in a way different from ours, but fun for him. Who is to say which game is right?

Chapter 35

ON INVESTING

You are your most valuable asset.

Almost everyone has access to information about investing financial resources to help insure a better financial future. The best investment is not stocks, bonds, real estate, precious metals or similar monetary instruments. The best investment you can ever make is in yourself.

Begin investing in yourself by purchasing a few books and reading them. Try a variety of subjects to help expand your mind and broaden your interests. No doubt you have always been curious about something. If you are interested in something, you can probably find a good book which will cover the topic of your interest. If you simply start with $100.00, you can easily acquire 5 to 6 good books. Pick one book which relates to your primary profession, try a book on self motivation, get one book on household financial investments, get a book about religion, the fifth book you should find is simply for your enjoyment. With these 5 to 6 books, give yourself half an hour to an hour to read each day. You will find the time spent very relaxing, and this information will help create new interests in life for you. Try sharing these new interests with someone you care about. You will find this sharing will give you one more way to enjoy yourself and your friends.

By reading about your primary job, you will surely discover ideas to help you. The more you know about your profession, and the more ideas you present to your employer the better income you can expect. Many employers will even reimburse you for the cost of the job related books you buy.

Once you start buying good books, keep every one and use them to start your own personal library. Over time, you will amaze yourself at the accumulation of books. If you do not have a separate room for your own library, buy a bookshelf, or use some space on a shelf in your closet for your library. The more you read the better person you will become and the more you will be likely to enjoy life.

Another investment you must make in yourself is by committing to a good diet and healthful exercise plan. Don't start a 10 day loose 30 pounds diet. Such crazy diet efforts often fail, resulting in a poor attitude about yourself. Use a simple diet plan sticking with the basics.

If you have the opportunity, see an exercise physiologist to get some ideas on exercise which will fit easily into your lifestyle. You shouldn't try to become Mister or Miss America your first time at a gym. A sensible exercise program doesn't have to cost you a bunch of money for designer exercise clothes, you don't even need a gym to exercise in! Walking is great exercise for nearly everyone. You can use a can of soup for a barbell to exercise your arms. Spending a lot of money will not make you physically fit, getting the right exercise for you is what matters. The time exercising is what matters.

Should you choose to pursue some form of exercise program make it something you can actually do, and try to enjoy your exercise program. Today there is far too much emphasis placed on exercise, causing many people to over exert themselves. Over exertion leads to pulled muscles, joint pain, and general physical distress. Develop an exercise program for you, don't let someone else dictate your exercise. Any time invested in exercise will help you maintain a healthier body which will result in a longer and more enjoyable life.

Once you have put together a good reading program to enhance your mind, and have a solid start to your diet and exercise program, it is time to move on to higher levels of personal development such as a financial plan, a plan of religious conviction, a family strategy, a career plan, and then put it all together for your own personal life plan.

For more help in developing a life plan for yourself, read through Maintaining Motivation, designing a balanced, successful life written by Matthew Mohr, copyright 2002.

As you move into a real life plan for yourself, you will find no end to the level of enjoyment you can derive from your life. Today you can only begin to imagine the great things which will occur in your life.

Chapter 36

YOUR PURPOSE

Set your sails properly, and you can go any direction you choose.

Why are you here on earth? A person with a sense of purpose for his life will be much more successful.

When you identify and pursue your purpose in life, you will become passionate about your life's activities. Troubles, trials, and tribulations will be overcome much easier because you will know you are building the life you desire.

Should you become passionate about a certain aspect of life and choose to pursue this aspect with all your effort, it should be enjoyable for you, provide benefit to society, and utilize the talents God gave you. Pursuing your life purpose will create a deeper sense of meaning for you, which will ultimately lead to a much happier life.

Thomas Edison pursued the creation of the light bulb with an unending passion. It has been reported that each time he tried a new bulb which didn't work, he considered his failed experiment another successful attempt to determine what wouldn't work. Through his passionate efforts, all humanity now enjoys the lights produced by his great invention.

In the early 1900's, few in this world could have predicted the rise and fall of Adolf Hitler, or the great impact of Sir Winston Churchill. Both men had passion and a compelling objective. Both inspired thousands to follow them, but one was following the right path, the other evil. Would the world be the same if Churchill had not believed it was his purpose to do right for England? Had evil (Hitler) prevailed; we would have a lot less happiness today.

Perhaps you do not see yourself possessing the talents or having a purpose as noble as Churchill or Edison, but how big your purpose in life is, is really up to you. No purpose is too big or too small.

Use your resources to pursue your purpose. Discover ways to enhance your life and the life of those around you through your purpose and ultimately you will succeed. Don't try to measure up to others expectations of how your life should be.

Chapter 37

JUST IMAGINE

Always imagine success, see your possibilities, and you will win.

We all are born with incredible imaginations, but somewhere along the way we choose not to use this great gift. Give a child a pencil, a piece of paper, a ruler, and a piece of string to play with. Most everyone quickly realizes a child with these four items would come up with a number of creations. Give the same items to a forty year old and you would probably get a laugh or a blank stare.

One can choose to maintain or even recreate a strong imagination. One day, as my friend Mark Bibelheimer, drove us in his car to lunch, my eye caught a note taped to his dashboard which said, "I am a creative genius". Upon inquiring what the note was all about, Mark told me he felt he had a lot of creativity he wasn't using, so to get out of his less creative mode, he wrote the note to remind himself to be as creative as possible. He also stated that since deciding to be more creative, his ability to find unique answers to puzzling questions went way up.

Just by reminding himself to be creative, Mark rediscovered his creative abilities. After hearing Marks idea, I decided to try it by simply telling myself frequently the same words as were written on Mark's note. It works!

Should you want a little more from your life, try using your creative mind powers. We all know yesterday is unchangeable, but we must all realize we can change tomorrow.

If you want to enhance your job, think about that job you wanted in the past but never got. Consider what it is about the job you didn't get which appears better than your current job. Start a list of things you can do in your current job which would make it seem more like your dream job, then take a chance on one or two of these ideas.

Many people feel trapped in a relationship which appears to be less than what they want. So often we hear (or think) about the one which got away. As we struggle with our current relationship we think of the one which got away, often believing this person would have been a better partner. If you are caught in this trap, consider if you could go back, make the change in relationship and determine how your life would be better and why. Use this exercise to determine how you need to change. Imagine you had made the changes and see your future as the way you want it. Use your imagination to project a brighter future, make some adjustments yourself, and you will find much of what you imagine will come true.

Imagination is very powerful. We cannot change the past, but we can change our future. Perhaps you've spent all your earnings and you are broke. If you have no financial resources, try to determine who convinced you that spending everything you earn is a good financial strategy. Money will not solve every problem, but if you consider your life closely, you may discover more financial possibilities than you think exist.

Chapter 38

YOU WIN A MILLION

The lottery counts on you, but you can't count on the lottery.

Pretend for a moment you unexpectedly receive one million dollars. You must put this one million to task by investing it, giving it away, paying debts, or buying things you want. It is your money to do with as you please.

Would this extra money help you pursue your defined purpose in life. If the money would lead to a successful life for you and a better society, you probably have a great idea worth pursuing.

Acting as a venture capitalist, in my work many great ideas have passed over my desk. In every venture, the passion of the person is gauged along with how much benefit society will receive from the venture before any investments are made.

Move away from your purpose to pure thoughts of enjoyment. Make a list of how you would dispose of this million dollars. How many items on the list are truly basic life needs for yourself? Your list probably includes very few necessities. This exercise is fun and can really help you grow an appreciation for the life you have. If you identify a number of things you want to do with this new money, use them as a launch pad for setting some goals for yourself so you can earn what you need to make these wants a reality.

Chapter 39

IF DEATH KNOCKED

Lilies look a lot nicer when you're looking down at them, then when you are buried beneath them.

The idea of death is not one to bring joy. If you knew in exactly one hour your life would end what would you do differently?

A very positive life changing exercise you can do is to seriously consider what changes you would make to your life and how this information would change what you do with the rest of your day if you knew you were going to leave this earth in one hour.

Were you too busy to embrace your spouse everyday, and if you were to know death was at hand, would you regret the lack of a daily embrace? Simple things like taking a minute everyday to tell those you truly love how you feel takes great commitment, but these little things lead to a much more joyful life.

Change the picture for a moment to knowing someone specific you love is going to die in one hour. How would you change your life and what would you do during this hour? Would you express your love for this person any differently knowing they were going to die? If this knowledge of impending death would compel you to change how you treat this person differently, why are you holding back? Take some action now to show real appreciation.

If you can identify anything significant or insignificant you would do differently each day should your time be limited, make a change and start doing what you know you should!

Chapter 40

CELEBRATE UNIQUENESS

There is only one you, and never will be another you.

We are all different in one way or another. We all differ in a lot of ways. Part of learning to live a more joyful life involves identifying your unique qualities and creating appreciation within yourself for your uniqueness. If you have ever known identical twins, you know they are different. One runs faster than the other. Perhaps one of these identical twins likes baseball, the other likes to go to movies. No two people are identical. Everyone is unique on this world and we all should look upon our differences as being special to us. Do not consider anything about you as unsightly or incomplete.

Many people claim that most, if not all, fashion models identify something about themselves as not perfect. People also claim once someone has surgery to correct a cosmetic defect, they often still see the defect, although it may be in a new way.

Perhaps my experience with fashion models has been unusual, for of the many female models I have know over the years, each of them had a very positive outlook and only one focused on what she perceived as a defect of her body. No one should believe the fallacy about not liking our personal attributes. You are made in God's own image. It's time you believe you are just the way you are supposed to be.

By taking on the opinion that differences amongst us and differences in nature can be fascinating, you can develop a much greater appreciation for life and find a lot of pleasure you may be missing.

Take a close look at a grassy meadow, be happy to discover the differences amongst the grasses which grow for you to enjoy.

Each blade of grass is different. Each feels different, each is a little different color, each a different length. Learn to enjoy the splendor of natural differences.

Closely look at your hairline. Do you see some differences in color between the strands of hair? Celebrate the differences! Think of how the combinations of each individual hair gives you your unique color. Perhaps you have no hair and you are bald. Consider yourself lucky for not having to clean up that mop top every morning!

Chapter 41

GETTING OUT
How much you put into something is far more
important than what you get out of something.

Should you wish to get more out of your life, you need to put more into your life. One simply can not expect to receive more from life than one puts into it.

As a life long student and teacher, the knowledge used in my life has only grown from rigorous study, interest in new material, and the application of information to life's problems.

Many times, even at the college level, students expect to get more from a class than the effort they are willing to put into the class.

Showing up for class at school doesn't entitle a student to a top grade any more than waking up in the morning entitles a person to a rewarding day. It is the effort the student makes and the efforts you make which determine the rewards.

Any type of relationship takes a commitment of continued effort in order for the relationship to succeed. In many ways, marriages which end in divorce occur today because one or both of the partners never really completely gave into the marriage.

When you start a new job, if you give your best effort to succeed in this new job, you are likely to enjoy your work. Far too often, people loose their excitement for their jobs resulting in a great loss to the person as well as their employer. People who stay with an employer for many years will most often be the company's greatest advocate. Long term employees find the good in their employers resulting in a happier work experience and generally resulting in better opportunities for the employee during his lifetime.

Most progressive employers are on the constant look out for people who show enthusiasm in their job, for people who go the extra mile to satisfy the customer, and present a positive image. As a result, the people who are enthusiastic, customer orientated, and positive, generally keep their jobs and earn a better income in comparison to their colleagues.

How much interest will you earn from your bank account until you first make some deposits of your own?

The formula is very simple; to get more out, put more in. The opposite formula holds as much power; you can't really ever get anything good out of something until you put something good into it.

Chapter 42

FIND GOOD

Most positive people look for and find the good in every experience. Looking for and accepting the good in your experiences takes hard work along with a commitment to look for the good.

We are not pretending nothing bad ever happens, but when a tragedy does occur, we need to search to find out what good resulted from this tragedy.

My son Benjamin has tremendous personal integrity. When we first started golfing, we allowed him some mulligans or redo's for his particularly bad shots. During February of 2002, we traveled to Arizona specifically to golf. Benjamin had his sights set on scoring a round of 18 holes below 100. As we completed the eighteenth hole of the second round during our Arizona trip, he shot a double bogie on a par 4 to give him a score of 101. He was really upset. After the round, we had a little talk about the reasonableness of a ten year old playing below 100 for a full round, and the fairness of mulligans. By mid June of 2002, he was consistently playing in the nineties. Then one day he said "Dad, how about we start playing the full eighteen with no mulligans for either of us?" We agreed the time had come for both of us to eliminate mulligans, so we started keeping a very strict score. We are now much more proud of our scores as we complete a game. Our scores reflect our skills, and a ten-year old determined for himself through experience what level of integrity he wanted for his life. Not surprising, he still hits in the nineties and gets upset at himself if he ever scores 100 or more. Certainly Benjamin's high level of integrity will lead him to a happier life. Benjamin discovered he was good enough to play a strict game by the rules.

Benjamin's integrity in the game of golf enhanced my opinion of him, and as a father, this gave me a great feeling of joy.

Chapter 43

QUICK SUMMARY

Life is made for living. The whole purpose of this book is to suggest to you that you can live the life you want and that a great life is available to you. By making changes to how you view life you can begin to really live!

Thank you for giving me some of your time, and take a chance on yourself today!

Chapter 44

IDEAS FOR YOU

Through the book a common set of themes emerged that you can use to enhance your long-term life. Implement them in your life and begin living better!

➢ If married, embrace your spouse at least once every day. If you can, embrace more than one time a day.

➢ Tell every member of your family that you love them everyday.

➢ Say a heartfelt thank you as often as you can.

➢ Learn to say you are sorry.

➢ Look for Gods gifts around you with awe.

➢ Read as much as you can.

➢ Ask questions and become interested in sharing ideas with others.

➢ Define and pursue what you like most.

➢ Change only to make your life and those you love better.

Chapter 45

BEGIN NOW

Today you can start appreciating life and enjoying your life more fully. Develop a sense of thankfulness for the world around you. Take some extra time to observe your world. Think about some good positive events in your life. Compliment a co-worker on anything they have done for you (Be sincere in your complement). Put on your favorite shirt. Do anything good which you think will add enjoyment to your day.

Start the process today, keep it up tomorrow, and see the positive results in your life. Start enjoying life. A good life for you is available as long as you take the chance on yourself!

Today and every day can be a great one for you!

Author Biography

Married, (Cynthia) three children, (Benjamin, Caleb, Berea).

Has a Bachelors Degree with Honors, in Economics and Business from North Dakota State University, and a Masters Degree from the Krannert Graduate School of Management, Purdue University.

Named one of five Krannert Scholars by the Krannert School faculty in 1983.

Employed by Texas Instruments, Dallas, Texas and Johnson City, Tennessee during 1983, 1984, and 1985.

Became Operations Manager of Dacotah Paper Company in June of 1985, became Vice President in 1987, Vice Chairman in 1990, President and Chairman of the Board in 1996.

Taught marketing at East Tennessee State University in 1984.

Taught finance, graduate marketing, and entrepreneurship at North Dakota State University during the 1980's, 1990's and 2000.

Director, Fargo Chamber of Commerce 1987 to 1992.

Director, Network Associates, Inc, Mount Prospect, IL, 1991 to 1997, completing his tenure as the Corporate Vice Chairman, having also served as Secretary to the Board and Corporate Treasurer.

Director, Vanity Stores during 1998 and 1999.

Director, MeritCare Foundation, 1994 to 2000, completing his tenure as Board Chairman in 2000.

Past President, NDSU Commons Club.

Authored and published multiple articles on Entrepreneurship.

Published Personal Riches and Entrepreneurship in 2001.

Published Maintaining Motivation in 2002.

Currently a Director for Community First National Bank of Fargo.

Currently serves as Audit Committee Chairman of Network Associates, Inc.

Presently a Director of the North Dakota State University Alumni Association.